Getting Started

Clicker
Training
for Cats

by Karen Pryor

A Karen Pryor
Clicker Book

Getting Started

Clicker Training
for Cats

by Karen Pryor

Sunshine Books, Inc.
49 River Street, Suite 3
Waltham, MA 02453-8345
www.clickertraining.com

Other titles in this series

Getting Started: Clicker Training for Dogs
by Karen Pryor

Getting Started: Clicker Training for Horses
by Alexandra Kurland

For information contact:
Sunshine Books, Inc.
49 River Street, Suite #3
Waltham, MA 02453
781-398-0754
www.clickertraining.com

Library of Congress Control Number: 2001117576

ISBN 1-890948-07-1
Book design by Codesign, Boston

Printed in the United States of America
10   9   8   7   6   5   4   3   2   1

Contents

Getting Started

Why train a cat?

This book is about a new way to have fun with your cat. It's called clicker training. Why would you want to try to train a cat? Everyone knows it can't be done. "Training cats" is an oxymoron. 'Herding cats' is a metaphor for trying to do the impossible. What would you train your cat to do—look beautiful? They know that. Stay clean in the house? Most cats are very careful about that. Would you want your cat to do dog-type tricks and wear funny hats? Certainly not. We respect cats for their dignity. How about being intelligent, affectionate, and amusing? They already are. Cats don't need training: that's one reason we enjoy their company. They come complete with everything they need to know. In fact, your cat probably trains you.

Clicking, however, is not really training as we usually think of it. It doesn't consist of commanding and obeying. It doesn't depend on social relationships such as dominance, or a desire to please. It's more like trading. Imagine that you're trying to strike a bargain with someone whose language you don't speak. You might use gestures and sounds to communicate "I'd like to buy that bracelet. I'll give you this much money." Clicking is like making a bargain. Since cats don't always recognize our gestures and noises, we use a clicker. The arbitrary click identifies what you like and promises to pay for it with something the cat likes.

That's all there is to it. The cat happens to jump off the table; you click, *during* the jump, and then give the cat a treat. Do it again a few times, and you'll have a cat that jumps off the table when it sees you coming. Don't want that? Okay, click as the cat happens to jump *on* the table; then give it a treat. After a few trades you can have a cat that jumps *onto* the table when it sees you coming.

When the cat seems confident about the plan, you can add a word or a gesture to indicate that the trading post is open and you're paying for jumps. Up! And the cat jumps up. Down! And the cat jumps down. *Click.* Amaze your friends.

The click can give you power to control your cat's behavior, and maybe sometimes you want that. But this is more than just a humane new way to keep a cat off the dining room table. (Or on the table, if you prefer.) It's really a way of communicating with another species. It's quick and easy for you. It's fun for the cat. The clicker game—for that's what it is, a powerful sort of game—can improve your cat's health, activity level, and attitude toward life. It can make your cat happier and more affectionate. By changing the cat's attitude it can also change the attitude of friends and family toward the cat. Above all—and this is what makes method worth trying—clicker transactions can help you and your cat develop a level of mutual communication, understanding, and esteem that you may never have imagined possible.

Improving a cat's daily life and attitude

Clicker training gives a cat—especially a housebound or apartment cat—something to do besides eat and sleep. Even the least little bit of time spent in clicker interactions, perhaps three or four minutes a day, will make changes in your cat. Aggressive, overactive animals calm down; couch potatoes rev up. In an elderly cat, clicker games can stimulate youthful playfulness and exploration once again. You know your cat can be amusing and personable; now you'll see that side of your pet more often, and so will your housemates, relatives, and friends.

The clicker game may also make your cat more interested in you. Did you ever have the feeling that you bore your cat? Does she ignore you until she hears the can opener? Does he sometimes run when you bend over to pick him up, struggle when you hold him, or duck when you offer a pat? Clicker games can change all that, not just because you hand out treats, but because you become an interesting challenge. The cat's part in the game is not to learn tricks, but to find ways to make you click so you'll give it a pat or a treat. From your standpoint you may be teaching the cat to come when called, or to roll over. From the cat's standpoint, it's training you to click; and that's very satisfying to cats.

In a way, the clicker game replaces the unavailable excitements of exploring and hunting in the wild. It gives the cat something interesting to do, not just with its agile body but with its far from insignificant intelligence. A 'clicker-wise' cat—one that has learned how to communicate through the game—may even initiate new clicker games with you, using its own creativity. (These are usually a lot more acceptable than finding new ways of making trouble, which the cat may enjoy and you may not.)

If your cat does have a behavior problem, clicker training can help (see Chapter Four, "Problems and Solutions"). But clicker training is not aimed at controlling behavior you don't like—it's designed to build new behavior. With this construction tool you can supplant old, unwanted behavior with new, desirable behavior; more than that, you can use your imagination—and your cat's—to find new things to do together, new ways to have fun. Clicker training is a way to enhance life for the cat and for you too.

What is clicker training?

Clicker training is the popular term for a science-based system called operant conditioning, using positive reinforcement and a marker signal to build new behavior. It's based on the way dolphins are trained. Dolphin trainers (who use a whistle, instead of a clicker, to identify behavior they want to encourage and shape) were the first to develop and expand this technology. Now, thanks to the Internet, clicker training is spreading to many species and uses all over the planet (see Chapter Five, "Resources"). Dog trainers are using clickers and positive reinforcers instead of old-fashioned choke collars and yanks on the leash. Horse owners are converting from spurs and whips to clicks and treats, to the relief and gratification of the horses. Zookeepers now use clicker training with all kinds of "untrainable" animals, from giraffes to polar bears, to facilitate handling and moving and veterinary care.

This is not traditional training. We clicker trainers don't order an animal around, or try to coax, lure, bait, or sweet-talk it into doing things. Instead we watch the animal and click when it does something we like, or when it takes a tiny step in the direction we have in mind. Then we give it a small treat. Then we wait and watch for the behavior to happen again.

The click (or some other arbitrary marker signal) is vital. It identifies the behavior you plan to pay for *in the instant that it's happening*. Animals really understand that because it's how they learn in nature. You tell the animal, "That's it! I'll pay you for exactly that!" every time you click. A food reward alone doesn't work this way; the only message of food by itself is "Yum." In fact, holding out food or waving it in the air actually distracts an animal from learning about its own behavior. And human-style praise, though welcomed by most cats, doesn't really pinpoint what earned that praise. The well-timed click, or some similar slightly startling event, identifies behavior with great accuracy. Establish a click and you have built a communication system.

Getting started

Clicker training begins with two things: some kind of desirable payment—usually but not necessarily food—and some kind of marker signal to identify the action you are paying for. For the latter you can use anything that makes a brief, sharp sound: flex the dimple in the lid from a baby food jar, click with a ball-point pen or a pocket stapler. Dolphin trainers use whistles. People with deaf animals use the blink of a flashlight. Experienced trainers and zoo keepers are partial to special training clickers, a sturdy version of the toy tin crickets children play with (see Chapter Five, "Resources").

Then you need treats. For your cat, it must be something that particular cat REALLY likes, not just something you think it likes or something you think is good for it. Most cats like diced ham, diced cheese, diced white meat of chicken, and, of course, tuna. If you don't know what your cat prefers, ask the cat by trying one thing at a time. The treat needs to be soft, so it can be eaten fast, and it needs to be something you can hand out in very small pieces: about pea-size is right for a cat. If you don't want to get food on the carpet or the furniture, use a little plate.

Each time you click, put the treat on the plate and let the cat eat it there. If you're worried about weight gain, substitute your training treats for ten to twenty percent of your cat's regular meals, and train before meals, not after.

What if your cat is on a restricted diet? Use preferred treats just at first, while you and the cat are learning the game. Then you can switch to the cat's regular food; just do your training immediately before you feed the cat, while it is hungry.

Commercial cat treats—dry, clean, and palatable— are handy to carry in your pocket if you want to treat the cat unexpectedly, but they are not ideal for clicker training. Most of them are so large that a cat will fill up after just a few pieces, and you may want to sustain the clicker game longer than just a few clicks. Most commercial treats also take quite a while to chew and swallow, during which time the cat may forget what it got clicked for. That's why fresh food is preferable, at least while you and the cat are beginning to learn the game.

Let's get going! Your first clicker session

Pick a time when your cat is hungry. Prepare ten to twenty little treats—morsels of cut up chicken, ham, or cheese is fine—and put them in a bowl. If you're going to present them on a plate, get the plate too. And get out your clicker.

I suggest that you begin your new clicker relationship by teaching the cat to touch a target. This is an easy behavior to build, and it has a lot of potential uses. A target can be any stick-like object, such as a pencil, a chopstick, or a wooden spoon. Sit down in a comfortable and familiar place where you and the cat often interact: in the kitchen, at the breakfast table, or on the living room couch.

If you have more than one cat, take the friendliest, hungriest one for your first subject, not the one with the most behavior problems. You're learning too—make it easy on yourself. Pick a moment when you and the cat can be alone; clicker work takes concentration, and other people will distract you. If you have other pets, shut them in another room, or take the cat you've chosen into the bathroom and shut the door.

Let the cat smell the treats, then put the bowl near you so you can reach it easily (and defend it from being raided, if necessary). Now pick up a treat, and *simultaneously click and give the cat the treat.* You can hand the treat to the cat, drop it on a plate, or just toss it in front of the animal. I like to toss the treat just far enough that the cat has to move a little to get it each time. Relax and do nothing while the cat eats the treat. Do this again four or five times. You're "charging up your clicker" by making the *click* mean "treat."

Don't try to touch the cat. Don't talk to it. Don't try to influence it in any way. It doesn't need to be looking at you and it doesn't need to be close to you to learn that "click means treats." Just click and treat. After a few simultaneous clicks, you can separate the click from the giving of the treat by half a second or so; click first, then treat (*not* the other way around).

Is the cat unresponsive?

During the first few sessions many cats walk away after only a few clicks and treats. That's fine; just stop there. Five clicks are a lot better than no clicks. The cat doesn't yet understand that these tidbits from heaven are not random events. It has no idea that it can control the game and keep it going, so it quits after the novelty wears off. Try again several hours later, or the next day. After a few sessions the cat will make the important discovery that some action of its own is actually making you click. Then it will want the game to go on longer.

What if your cat eats only one or two treats and then seems to lose interest? You might think your cat "doesn't like" clicker training, or that the clicker "doesn't work." In fact the commonest cause of disinterest is free feeding. If your cat has food in the form of dry kibble available at all times, it probably doesn't have room in its stomach for more than one or two treats. The first step is to take the dry food away for two or three hours before you have a clicker session. Then you may want to rethink your feeding program (see "Making treats more desirable").

Shaping the first behavior

Let's suppose that your cat has become quite interested and wants more treats. Take up the target and hold it an inch or two in front of the cat. The cat is highly likely to look at the end of the target stick or even to sniff it. (To make sure of this, you can rub a little food on the stick to make it smell good.) Click as the cat's nose touches the stick, then put the target out of sight and give a treat. The instant the cat finishes chewing, hold the target stick out again. (Do you feel as if you need three hands, one for the clicker, one for the target, and one for the treats? Try holding the target and the clicker together in one hand.)

Most cats will nose the end of a stick almost automatically; I think this is related to a natural scent-marking behavior. If the cat just stares at the target the first time, move it very close to the cat's nose, so it almost *has* to touch it. Click and treat, then instantly offer the cat the opportunity to touch the target again. You want the cat to earn each click by doing something, even if it's just turning its face toward the target, but you want to make the job easy enough to keep those clicks and treats coming.

Now try offering the target at a slight distance, so the cat has to move toward it a step or two. Animals seem to realize more easily that their own actions are causing the click if they are moving when they hear it. If the cat is sitting or doesn't move toward the target, toss or hold out a treat so the cat has to come forward to eat it. Then offer the target again while the cat is in motion.

Click the cat *at the instant it touches the target*, not afterward. One great advantage of using the click instead of, say, the word "Good" is that it provides instant feedback for you as well as for the cat. If you click *after* the cat bumped the target, you'll hear the difference and realize you were a little late; it's much harder to identify and correct your own timing errors if you're using a word.

How long is the session?

Five minutes is plenty at first. The cat is in charge. You can sometimes click a dog or a horse a hundred times in a given session and they'll still want more, but cats seem to work best in short spurts. Some owners find that even a major, extended session with an experienced, hungry cat won't go much beyond twenty clicks and treats.

No matter how much or how little you have accomplished, your first session is a big step. Don't be in a hurry to repeat the thrill. Research shows that in both animals and people it takes some hours for newly learned information to cross over into long-term memory. Let the new information sink in for a few hours, even overnight, before you try again.

Ending the session

Ideally, you want to quit while the cat is still interested, but at first this is in part a matter of luck. If the cat tires before you do, and turns its back and starts washing its face, don't take it personally. The cat is done and so is the session. Put everything away and plan another session for later on or the next day. Every click counts, so even if you've gotten in only a few clicks, you and the cat have made permanent progress. Respect the cat's right to end the experience. Trying to coax, lure, or pressure an animal into just one more repetition is frustrating for both of you. You can't "make" the cat want to work, and if you try to do so the cat may find your efforts aversive and decide that clicking is not that much fun after all.

Once you've gotten as far as offering the target, be careful not to leave your target lying around where the cat can get to it while you're not looking. The cat may touch it, hear no clicks, feel disappointed, and scorn the target when you bring it out next time. When he's more experienced he won't make that mistake, but in the beginning cats are easily discouraged by this kind of mishap. Also, refrigerate your treats immediately. Cats are very sensitive about stale food; in fact, you may find it's better to discard leftover treats and prepare fresh ones for each session.

More target training

Sooner or later, after one session or five, your cat will be approaching the target with vigor, bumping it, and maybe swatting at it with a paw. See if you can get it to follow a moving target a step or two. Let the cat catch up, touch, and get clicked. Next, take the cat a little further, two or three feet maybe. Can you lead the cat back and forth? Great! How about across the table top, or across your lap if you're on the couch, or around a chair leg if you're on the floor. Is the cat following? *Click.* You have just developed the behavior clicker trainers call targeting.

Targeting has a lot of uses. You can use your target stick to get the cat to jump up onto a piece of furniture, or to get it to leap down. You can have the cat jump over your arm just for fun, or from one chair or stool to another. You can play "chase and catch" games with the target. You can target the cat into its carrying case and out again. You can transfer the targeting behavior to your fingertip, and then use your finger to guide the cat wherever you like.

Perhaps sometime you will really need the cat to do something it doesn't want to do—come out from under the bed on moving day, for example. Even if the cat is far too stressed to care about food, your target may do the trick all by itself. And there's another good reason to start your clicker experience with targeting. Clicker trainers have learned that the very first behavior an animal learns to do for a click is apt to become very persistent. If that first behavior is something the animal can do on its own—spinning in a circle, say—it's likely to crop up whenever the animal is confused about how to get you to click. Clicker trainers call this the default behavior, and its persistence can get in the way of learning other skills. Targeting, however, depends on the presence of a target; by bringing out the target or putting it away you control the default behavior.

Catching something cute

Clicker training doesn't always have to be a project. One of the most delightful things to do with the clicker is just reward your cat for the amusing little things cats do on their own. How do you begin? Keep a clicker handy and notify the cat when it's doing something cute. Keep a few dry treats in your pocket or in a jar in each room, so you have something with which to pay the cat.

What do you click? Anything. The cat rolls over? *Click.* The cat pats a ball and sends it rolling? *Click.* The cat leaps sideways? *Click.* The cat chases its tail? *Click!* To get the hang of the timing, pretend you're taking a photograph of the action: try to click while the cat is doing the thing, not after it has stopped. You can also use your clicker to select little pieces of natural actions and, as it were, freeze-frame them. For example, while the cat is washing its face you can catch the moment the paw goes behind the ear, click that, and begin to isolate the behavior of putting a paw behind one ear and holding it there. After a few repetitions you have a cat that looks as if it were trying hard to hear a faint sound. (Clicker training is useful, but having fun is important too, for both you and your cat.)

What happens when you surprise a cat with a click and treat for something it's doing on its own? At first the cat will just look mystified, collect or ignore its treat, and go on about its business. But take notice: across a period of days, the thing you have "captured" will begin to occur more often. By and by the cat will begin doing the behavior on purpose, hoping to make you click. "See me? I'm rolling over." "See me? I'm doing my sit." Good! *Click!*

Clicking without a clicker

What if your cat does something adorable and you don't have a clicker and treats handy? You can make a click sound with your tongue—trainers call it a mouth click. It won't have quite the same penetrating effect, but the fact that you marked the behavior as it happened will allow the cat to remember what it did, even if you have to go to the kitchen to actually produce the treat. Marking the action as it happens is the crucial element.

You can also spend an occasional treat on deliberately establishing a vocal signal such as the word "Good!" or "Yes." The trouble with using a word or phrase to mark the behavior you like is that it we humans tend to get careless with words; we use them in regular conversation, which may seriously diminish their meaningfulness to the cat. Also, we are apt to speak the word slowly, too late, or not at all. It may seem counterintuitive, but in fact, whether beginners or long-time trainers, we are all much more consistent with a clicker than with language. Even so, a mouth click or a spoken word is always available, and some kind of marker is better than none.

Fear of the clicker: A temporary problem

Some cats react to any new sound by being startled. If your cat seems afraid of the clicker, muffle the device in your hand or pocket, or wrap it in a towel temporarily. You also soften the clicker sound by putting several layers of duct tape or electrical tape over the dimple in the metal spring. Don't point the clicker at the cat as if it were a TV remote—that would make anyone nervous. If the cat flees, don't chase him or to drag him out of his hiding place to force him to accept the clicking. Take two or three days to pair the sound of a quiet click with good events like dinnertime, petting, play, and homecoming. Give the cat a chance to discover that clicks mean good things. Once you start the actual training, the cat will make a second big discovery: that he can make you give him treats by making you click. Then he'll come to love the sound.

Making treats more desirable

Some beginning clicker trainers discover that their cat isn't interested in the treats offered, or eats one or two and then leaves. Sometimes the cat just doesn't have the picture yet, and sometimes you do have to experiment to find a treat that your cat particularly favors. But the most common reason for a cat spurning a treat is that it's not interested because it's not hungry.

Do you leave food down all the time for your cat? Some people believe this is how cats should be fed: the "real dinner" is moist cat food given once or twice a day, but dry kibble should be available at all times. In fact, constant availability of food is actually biologically inappropriate for cats. Cats are not grazers that have evolved to nibble on pastures all day. They are small-prey predators, and one or two meals a day is much more suitable to their insides.

People observe that most cats stop eating when they're full and often leave food behind, unlike most dogs, who will bolt down everything available. We can't assume from that, however, that a cat is wise about how much it eats across a period of time. A cat may fill up quickly, but it can fill up over and over and over in a day. One can easily identify the cat that is fed *ad libitum*, as the vets say. First, it is never very hungry, so even the most delicious treats may get only cursory attention. Second, it is likely to be obese. Naturally an obese cat is apt to have a poor appetite at any given moment—it's already full.

Do you think your cat is just a really big cat, not actually overweight? Try this test. Put your hands around the cat's rib cage, right behind its elbows, so your fingers touch underneath and your thumbs touch or overlap on top. Now slide your hands backwards to the hips. Does the circle get bigger as you move back? Yes? Then your cat is fat.

If your cat seems heavy, or is uninterested in treats, try an experiment. Take away the kibble bowl. Feed twice a day. Ten minutes after each feeding remove any food the cat hasn't eaten. Do some clicker training before meals. Mark down on paper how many behaviors you clicked in each session. You will almost certainly record a conspicuous change by the end of the first week.

Now keep up this feeding program for the rest of the cat's life—a life that will most likely be longer, more active, and healthier than the cat had any chance of under the previous regime.

Alternatives to food treats

Perhaps your cat is on a special diet for medical reasons, or perhaps you've been told that it's wrong to use food in training. You can, of course, use anything the cat enjoys, such as petting or brushing, as a reward associated with the click. You can also use toys and play. But learning is likely to proceed much more slowly when using a physical activity as a payoff. The activity takes up time, and by the time the cat finishes playing or being petted it may have forgotten what it got clicked for. In addition, the cat may tire of the reinforcer after three or four presentations.

It really is best to use food, at least at the beginning. Food treats will give you some quick and early successes, and that's important for both you and the cat. If things go too slowly you might each lose interest before you really catch on to the game. The amount of food your cat will consume in tiny treats is minor compared to its regular meals, and insignificant when weighed against the possibility of a lifetime of improved activity levels and an improved relationship with you and the rest of the household.

If you must feed the cat only its prescribed diet, use that food (in tiny bites presented on a spoon) and have your training session right before dinnertime. Finally if you must "free feed," take the dish away at night and train first thing in the morning. Or take it up for at least three hours before you start a session.

Starting a clicker log

Since cats often learn in short spurts, it's good for your training and important for your morale to jot down what happened in each session. This will be especially useful if you started out with any kind of food problem; you may need written evidence, just at first, to really see your progress.

Keep track of your sessions in a notebook. How many clicks? For what behaviors? It's handy to have some kind of simple record of what behaviors you are working on; that way you won't disappoint the cat if it suddenly makes a breakthrough. Also, progress that isn't obvious to you on a daily basis shows up much better on paper. When you feel you're not getting anywhere with a particular behavior, it's encouraging to look at earlier logs and see how far you have come.

How fast can you go?

Sometimes cats catch on to clicker training with mind-boggling speed. A professional dog trainer of my acquaintance went home from one of my seminars still feeling doubtful. The next morning, in a few minutes of clicking she trained her cat to follow a teaspoon all around the breakfast table. That week, she told me later, she converted her entire dog school to clicker training.

I also heard from a cat owner who happened to be housebound with a broken leg when she decided to try the clicker with her cat. In her first session she trained her cat to follow a pencil across the couch, and then, using the pencil as a target, to jump through an embroidery hoop.

Another beginner reported on the Internet cat clicker list that in her first ten-minute session she succeeded in getting her cat to jump onto the top of the chest-type freezer in the kitchen (out of range of the household dogs), station herself on a little step-stool on the freezer, and then sit up in a begging position like a dog. An hour later, the woman's husband was in the kitchen snacking on some cold fried chicken and lo and behold, the cat was doing her "sit up" on the stool—she definitely wanted a piece of that chicken. (The owner wrote in her post, "Yes, my hubby did reinforce it.…He had to…she was tooo cute.") In that first session the cat had learned a lot more than just how to get a piece of chicken. She had learned a whole new communication system—*much* more effective with humans than old-fashioned meowing—and she was putting it right to work.

Useful Behavior

If you and your cat have broken the ice with targeting, you now know how to play the clicker game together. What else could you teach your cat to do? Here are some practical things you can teach your cat with the clicker:

- *To come (reliably) when called*

- *To stop mewing and twining around your legs while you're cooking*

- *To walk on a leash outdoors*

- *To wait to be picked up*

- *To be gentle with teeth and claws*

- *To permit grooming and handling without a struggle*

In this chapter we'll look at these clicker projects one by one, and we'll discuss clicker training in the multiple-cat household.

What if you have a behavior problem that's not on this list? The basic techniques and principles you learn while building a useful behavior can often help you discourage one you don't like. And because boredom and lack of stimulation are the cause of many problem behaviors, just introducing the mental stimulation of clicker training can make for dramatic changes: often misbehavior just fades away. I'll discuss some common behavioral problems and suggested solutions in Chapter Four; here we'll consider training projects aimed at simplifying and enriching your life with your cat.

Come when called

Dogs are always hoping you have something for them. It's fairly easy to get most dogs to come when called. Cats—famously—don't necessarily care if you have something for them or not, and are capable of ignoring "Here, kitty, kitty" for hours. If they're apprehensive in new surroundings or feel threatened they can be even harder to retrieve: their impulse to come to you may be swamped by fear. (I was at a friend's New York apartment once when her cat slipped out the door unnoticed: it took us hours to find her, lost and bewildered, crouched in a corner of an unused stairwell three floors down.)

A clicker-wise cat, on the other hand, has learned to regard your signal to come as an opportunity to command a performance from you. "I shall appear at your feet, and you will immediately click and pay me. Good person." With the clicker, therefore, you have a better chance of teaching a cat to come to you reliably even under tricky circumstances.

I live in a city house, on the ground floor, so for safety's sake, my kitten, Mimi, is an apartment cat. But I know she could escape to the outdoors; in fact, though I am vigilant, I'm sure she will get out someday. This is why the first thing I taught her was a cue meaning "come here right now." For me it was the most important safety training I could give her. We practice it almost every day, in different areas and different circumstances. If I come across some especially interesting treat for her, I take the opportunity of using it to reinforce this most important behavior.

In this case Mimi's cue is the phrase, "Mimi, come!" Trainers call this a recall signal. When Mimi hears her recall signal she comes to me at a run, even if she's been asleep. I've used my recall to find Mimi when she went exploring in the basement, and to get her home when she escaped up the back stairs to my neighbor's apartment.

Teaching cues

Teaching "Come" is not exactly like teaching targeting. In that case we developed a behavior that didn't exist previously, then we shaped the behavior of following a stick, step by step. What we need to build in this case is not the behavior but a reliable response to your signal. The cat already knows how to come over to you to be petted or fed. Now we are going to build a cue of some kind that causes the behavior to happen when you want it to, not just when the cat decides it's convenient.

There already exists a traditional clicker cue for calling cats: two sharp raps on the nearest firm surface. On my video, *Clicker Magic,* a collection of clicker sessions between a variety of trainers and animals, clicker trainer Catherine Crawmer, founder and editor of *American Animal Trainer* magazine, uses a double rap on a table to call her cat, Wendy, at which point the cat comes from out of view at a dead run and leaps up onto the table. Impressive. Now a lot of cat trainers use the same cue, even me. My dogs know "Come," but only Mimi knows the rap-rap cue. It allows me to call the cat without bringing the dogs running, which is sometimes a convenience.

It doesn't matter what the sound is; think of the cats who come running when they hear the can opener. Any sound becomes important if it constitutes the announcement that a particular behavior—running toward the sound—will result in something good to eat. (For a step-by-step process for assigning a cue to a behavior, see Chapter Three, under "Naming behaviors").

A recall signal needs to be maintained and strengthened at every opportunity. A successful recall should NEVER go unreinforced. If the cat comes, you need to be ready with a treat or, at the very least, a pat. Whether you are using your voice, a rap, or some other cue, use the same cue every time, and use it just once—don't teach the cat that it can successfully wait for the fourth or fifth call and still get reinforced when it shows up.

You can strengthen your signal by using it during normal household activities. Whenever there's an opportunity to call your cat—as you come home from work, when you're going to give the cat its dinner, when you feel like having a clicker session—give your cue and click the cat as it comes toward you. Then treat. Each time you can get the sequence to occur—you give a single recall cue, the cat comes running, you click while it's moving toward you, and something good happens for the cat—you're building more power into that cue. And the treat need not be food, of course. A new toy or a play session with you is a fine payoff for coming when called.

If you have an older cat who is well accustomed to ignoring you, this may take time. The cat's most likely been fooled before: perhaps "Here, kitty, kitty" did not lead to a delicious chicken liver, but to a trip to the veterinarian. In that case you need a new cue, not the old words you've always used. Try Catherine's rap-rap; that will keep you clear about using a new cue. In two or three days you should see the response to the cue beginning to strengthen: the cat comes more often, starts to come more promptly, and comes on the run.

A "Come" cue also makes for a nice game. You can play hide and seek with your cat, even in a small apartment. Step into the closet, give the cue, and click and treat the cat for finding you. Try harder places. Get a child or other friend to play with you, and call the cat back and forth between you, clicking and treating at each end. The click sounds the same no matter who makes it, so the cat "believes" the new person's clicker right away and responds with alacrity, usually to the great enjoyment of your helper. Involving other people is fun for everyone and widens the cat's circle of trusted friends as well.

Keep the game lively. Try to quit before the cat wants to stop, remembering that one or two or three successful recalls constitutes a perfectly fine training session for a cat. If the cat begins to lag, either stop the session or make things a little more interesting. For example, at first you and your friend could cue the cat back and forth a few feet between you, then from room to room, then from different parts of the house. Use a jackpot reward now and then, such as the cat's dinner or a catnip mouse. Keep the cat winning—don't make the game so hard there's no chance of getting a click. But also keep the cat guessing— "What are they going to come up with next?" It's good for cats to have something to think about.

What if you have more than one cat? Concentrate on one, but give a treat to any of the others that begin responding to the cue. Cats love to learn by watching each other, and you get two educated cats for the price of one. And by the way: never use your clicker itself to call cats. Yes, that does work initially: the sound of the click brings the cats running because they want to play the clicker game. But you weaken the clicker for other behavior if you use it as a cue or trigger for "Come." The cat expects to be reinforced simply for being nearby, and may take up begging instead of learning new responses.

Places, please: The alternative to begging

All the cats I've ever lived with encouraged food preparation every way they could—usually by meowing, twining around my legs, tripping me, and getting in my way while I was trying, darn it, to fix their food. Once, my daughter Gale, then fourteen, walked into the kitchen and caught me in the act of booting an especially irritating cat across the floor. "Mom!" she cried. "What are you *doing?* You're an animal trainer!" Yes indeed. We dolphin trainers know that punishment is never necessary and seldom productive: any behavior the animal is capable of can be reliably developed with a marker signal and a treat. So how to stop this nuisance behavior through positive reinforcement?

My solution was to give that cat, and every cat I've owned since, a special place in which to wait for dinner. The cat's job is to sit in that spot until I click or say "Okay," and put its dinner dish down.

It's easy to teach this behavior to cats (harder with dogs). You can get a good start on it the first time you try. Wait for dinnertime. (There's an advantage of feeding cats on a schedule. Dinnertime becomes anticipated, in the cat's stomach and in its brain, which makes the cat very willing to learn new things for food at that hour.)

Fix the cat's dinner, set it aside, and get out the treats. Small pieces of the impending dinner will do, or you might begin with something special. Choose a place where the cat can see you but won't be in your way: perhaps a kitchen stool. (Cats feel safer off the ground. They also enjoy watching what people are doing, and a higher perch improves the view.)

Don't pick the cat up and put it on the stool. The cat learns nothing from that except to wait to be picked up. Instead, use a target or a bit of food to lure the cat. As the cat jumps up on the stool, click, then give the treat. Now pause. Count to three. If the cat is still sitting on the stool, click and treat. When the cat finishes chewing, count to five. Is the cat still there? Click and treat again.

Don't talk to the cat while you do this, and don't move around during these first few clicks. You don't want the cat to be looking for hints, in your voice or body language, about when the treat is coming. Counting to yourself, gradually extend the time you require the cat to stay on the stool, aiming for a successful wait of fifteen seconds. Now surprise the cat by throwing in a really easy three-second wait. (It's a good idea to mix in a short wait now and then—you don't want the cat to think the job always gets harder and harder.) After the short wait, click and instead of giving a treat, set the cat's dinner dish on the floor, step back, and let the cat have its meal.

That's the first lesson. At the next mealtime, repeat the first lesson, but move away from the cat now and then, touching things on the counter, maybe opening the refrigerator. You're communicating, "Stay on the stool to get clicked, even if I'm doing things elsewhere in the kitchen." If the cat jumps down, lure it back up and go back to standing in front of it, count again, and click and treat. (Use short counts, three seconds, then five, then ten, when refreshing the rules after an error. Make it easy for the cat to succeed, so it can catch on to the new rule quickly.)

Staying longer and longer

Training this behavior introduces us to another elegant aspect of clicker work: building the duration of a behavior. Now the cat knows how to sit on a stool. All you need to do is stretch out the length of time you require it to do so. If you do this methodically, in the first two lessons you will successfully communicate to the cat, "Sometimes you have to wait longer than other times, but I will always pay you if you do stay there."

You can then go from actually watching the cat, counting the seconds, and clicking to randomly glancing at the cat as you move around the kitchen, occasionally saying a praise word or phrase such as "Good kitty" and giving a small treat now and then. Most cats will continue to sit there, waiting for the sporadic small payments, until you give the big jackpot, the actual dinner. Cats understand waiting: that's one way they hunt. Going to one's place and waiting is a behavior that rapidly builds itself.

What if the cat is mewing and otherwise making a fuss on the stool? Just be careful you don't mark that behavior accidentally. Make your click in an instant of silence, however brief, and during instances of sitting rather than pacing and turning. Usually the begging behaviors will drop out in favor of quiet sitting if they are not accidentally reinforced. Soon the cat will have the behavior down pat. "Sitting still, in this place, makes my person give me my dinner." Now you can drop out the intermediate treats and maintain the behavior with just one reinforcer, the dinner bowl itself.

After some weeks or months, or (more likely) after you've gotten careless about what you are actually reinforcing, the behavior may deteriorate a little, with the cat jumping down before you have given your okay signal. In that case just rebuild the behavior by reviewing the original shaping. Go back to reinforcing sporadically with small treats while the cat is on the stool, using just a word or phrase—"Yes" or "Good cat"—as a marker, with the click only at the end.

The "Places, please" behavior, static though it might seem, can be a lot of fun to watch. A few years after the infamous booting incident I found myself living in a New York apartment with three cats: Gale's beautiful Burmese, Tosca; Beebee, a marmalade stray my son Mike had rescued from the streets as a kitten; and Manon, a surly black female we had adopted from the local shelter. When I stood up and headed for the kitchen around six p.m., those cats, electrified, appeared from wherever they were, raced ahead of me, and hit their respective kitchen chairs hard enough to slide them into the wall with a bang.

There they sat while I got out the bowls, opened the cans, added the vitamins and leftovers, stirred it all up, apportioned it, put it down on the floor—and finally said, "Okay." Then the cats hit the floor and bolted their anticipated dinners with gratifying appetite.

Of course even a cat sitting totally still can project strong feelings. While I prepared their meals, three pairs of cat eyes pierced me with a fixed, maniacal glare, willing me to move faster: "Hurry, hurry, hurry." Their total buy-in to the plan was hilarious and also touching. They did not beg or bother me when I was cooking at other times. They believed I was going to feed them at or near six o'clock every day. They believed that holding tight to their places was what would make me do it. And they were right.

Walking on a leash

Dr. Nicholas Dodman, a noted veterinarian and behaviorist, maintains in his book *The Cat Who Cried for Help* that cats are only truly happy if they can have free access to the outdoors. Unfortunately, for city dwellers that is not an option. And even if you live in the suburbs or the countryside there are always the dangers of traffic, rival cats, stray dogs, coyotes, and, of course, parasites, fleas and ticks, and contagious cat diseases.

If yours is fated to be an indoor cat—for whatever reason—you still might like to take it outside sometimes, if only for the pleasure of a new experience. One safe way to do so is on a leash. People assume you can't teach a cat to accept a leash, but really it's just that you can't treat them like dogs. The traditional way of training dogs to walk on a leash, using voice commands and a "corrective" jerk on the collar, is disastrous with cats. Their only response to an aversive stimulus is fight or flight, and they quickly learn to hate and fear the whole process. Secondly, cats' necks are much more vulnerable than dogs' necks; jerking or pulling on a cat's collar is not only distressing to the cat, it's dangerous. But there is another way.

Before you take your indoor cat outside, make sure its shots are up to date. You may also want to ask your veterinarian about flea repellents. Then get your cat a harness. Most pet stores carry soft woven nylon harnesses, suitable for cats, ferrets, and other small animals. The harnesses adjust easily and seem to be quite comfortable; many cats accept them without apparent objections right from the start, and most get used to them fairly quickly.

Next, attach a light six-foot line to the harness and let the cat drag it around the house for a while. Eventually the line is bound to get tangled up on something. You come along and untangle it. You can use a click or a word to tell the cat that it can move freely again, or you can just let the situation sink in by itself.

Soon the cat will discover on its own that the leash, by and large, is harmless. But it will learn that it has to stop when the line becomes taut, or at least to stay within the area limited by the leash. The cat will also discover that you are the miracle worker who can give it freedom to move again. Repeat the experience for short periods (fifteen minutes) over several days, or until the cat seems completely comfortable.

On your first excursion outside, hold the leash and follow the cat as she ventures into the unknown. If she's petrified, and wants to run inside again, let her. That's your first session. If she just wants to crouch and stare, that's okay too. She's safe because you have the leash and she can't get far if she panics, and she's learning, just by looking and smelling and hearing, about this new world. If she starts exploring, fine. Go with her. Let her choose where this first walk will go.

If she tries to venture someplace you don't think is safe — under the house, say, or into the street — just stand still, letting the line become taut, until she turns in another direction. Then you click or use a praise word and go with her again. The indoor desensitization period should have forestalled any tendency to struggle against the leash.

Once the cat is accustomed to this, you can use a much longer line and give her quite a bit of leeway to explore. The Clintons took their cat, Socks, for walks around the White House grounds on a lightweight thirty-foot line. That's long enough so that a cat has quite a lot of freedom. And even in an emergency, if the cat were to take off at a dead run, you have time to step on the line to stop her, and the harness can absorb the jolt of an emergency halt without hurting the cat as a collar might.

Tinsley Ginn, an Atlanta cat owner, desensitized her cat to the restriction of the leash in the house, and then started taking her for walks. Instead of just following the cat around, she clicked and treated the cat for coming toward her and for staying with her when she was moving. The cat now walks briskly in front of her, as a dog might, and when last heard from they had extended their daily travel distance to three blocks.

The pickup cue

There will be times when you want or need to pick up your cat. First learn to pick up it in a cat-friendly way. Some people pick up cats (and puppies) by grabbing them around the middle and hoisting them with all four legs dangling, often when the animal doesn't expect it. No animal likes this. Cats sometimes put up with it because they put up with a lot of stuff from us (docility is a price they pay for living in our houses), but sometimes they learn to duck and run when they see a hand coming.

Instead, always pick your cat up fore and aft, and immediately support its legs so they don't dangle. If your cat resists, here's a great place for a click-and-treat repair job. Off and on during the week, especially right before dinner, pick up the cat, click any sign of relaxing, release the cat immediately, and treat. Eventually you can substitute stroking in a favored spot, such as under the chin, as the reinforcer for relaxing. When the cat accepts being lifted and held, you can start adding a cue such as the words "Pick up time" that tells the cat what to expect. Being lifted then becomes a cued behavior. The cat hears the cue and automatically stands still to be lifted.

Now when you're faced with possible danger outdoors, or when you're in a stressful environment like the vet's office, you can tell your cat that you're going to pick him up and that he needs to stay quiet in your arms. The chances are good that the cat will trust the information and gladly let you hoist him to safety and/or hold him, rather than taking matters into his own hands and scratching or running away.

Gentle paws

"Help! My cat plays too rough! She's scratching and biting me!" Veterinarians hear this all the time. Some people, unwittingly, actually train this behavior. They don't want to punish, so they do nothing when their cat bites or scratches in play (for scratching in fear or anger, see Chapter Four, "Problems and solutions"). The cat, assuming the person is playing too, may get rougher and rougher, to the point of drawing blood, without any idea that she is offending.

The cat plays with you as she would with another cat. As she reaches adolescence and then adulthood, that play might get rougher. You are a thin-skinned human being without protective fur, but she doesn't know that—you have to teach her. Here's how: the instant she pricks you with a claw or lays teeth on your skin, get up and walk away. You won't be hurting her feelings, you'll just be teaching her that one behavior, soft paws, prolongs playtime, and others, clawing or biting, puts an end to it.

Maine Coon cats and other cats with extra toes sometimes have non-retracting claws; most cats, however, have voluntary control over their claws. They can extend them on purpose, and they can perfectly well learn not to. Just as you should learn to pick up your cat gently, she should learn to keep her claws in and her mouth shut when she is playing with people. You're providing a consequence for behavior—not a punishment, just an end to the fun. If she wants to be within touching distance, she has to touch politely. When she jumps into your lap with soft paws, or pats your hand gently, praise and pet her. If she jumps into your lap with her claws out, put her back on the floor.

You can give praise and pats or clicks and treats for retracted claws in many different situations. When the cat rides on your shoulder without digging in with her claws, or plays softly with toys, your clothes, your hand, or your toes under the blankets, you can let the play continue, or even reward her with pats, clicks and treats. On the other hand, if you tolerate rough play by being "being nice" to the cat and enduring more and wilder activity, you are actually teaching her to get rougher and rougher. Your choice.

Grooming and handling

Probably your cat already enjoys being petted, and perhaps being brushed as well. But are there parts of the body it won't let you touch? Many cats resist having their bellies stroked, for instance. What if someday your cat had a wound there, or a burr working its way into the skin? What if it had a thread or wire caught in its teeth, or a broken, bleeding claw? What if it developed a tumor? You would want to be able to examine the area, so at the very least you could take the cat to the vet and say, "Look at this," without the vet having to anaesthetize the cat just to see what the problem might be. (Vets will tell you this is sometimes necessary.)

So you need to be able to touch your cat all over, including opening and looking inside its mouth, handling its paws, turning it upside down and feeling its stomach without resisting. The experienced long-time animal person, a breeder, say, will start when the animal is very, very small, picking it up, putting it down, handling it all over, turning it on its back, looking in its the mouth, and so on. By the time the animal is six weeks old, being handled has become part of life, perhaps (ideally) even enjoyable.

If, however, your cat is not totally blasé about being touched and handled, the clicker will help. Here's a great time to establish that the clicker doesn't just mean food but other kinds of good things as well. Find out where your cat loves best to be stroked: from chin to chest, under the jaw, is popular; from head to tail along the back is good; the base of the tail is another favorite spot. Some cats like to be scratched behind the ears. Some really love to be gently massaged along the big muscles of the back and upper legs. So there are your reinforcers. Since you need both hands to do this, make a click sound with your mouth, or use verbal praise with these reinforcers.

Now, calmly, when the cat is in your lap and you are both relaxed, handle a resistant area—paws, mouth—briefly, then click and immediately stroke a favorite area. This is a nice evening game to play, with the cat in your lap as you watch TV. As you hold that paw or feel inside that lip, give your click sound or praise word the moment the muscles under your hand relax, even a little. (Sensitive ears are often a sign of ear infections. Check with the vet if your cat resists having its ears rubbed).

Besides praising and stroking, you should release the pressure by backing off a little or letting go entirely, when you click. This is another way of rewarding the cat for non-resistance. He discovers that he can make you stop touching a sensitive area, at least momentarily, by relaxing. So he learns to relax more and more, while you handle him more and more freely.

One useful outcome of shaping handling is that one can clip the cat's nails. I trim off the sharp little tips of Mimi's fast-growing claws every few days, while I'm watching the evening news. She seems to consider her manicure a pleasant luxury. I sort of enjoy it too, because her soft relaxed paws are so cuddly, and it vastly reduces snags in my clothing and pinpricks in me.

Training multiple cats

How do you do all this if you have more than one cat? Here's some good advice from Wendy Jeffries, a pioneering cat clicker trainer and owner of the on-line cat clicker list:

> I always recommend starting with the most food-motivated beast of the bunch, whether it is dogs, cats or birds. You will learn a lot working with that first eager animal and will then be better prepared to instruct the others. It's lots easier to remember where you left off [when you begin with] only one.

> You will make all your mistakes with the first kitty and the next ones will have the benefit of an experienced teacher. Also remember those mistakes made in clicker training are usually easily corrected with more clicker training. That's the best thing about clicker training. There's no negative fallout like there is with punishment-based training. The worst that happens is we may unintentionally train something. For instance you might get a "sit pretty" with paws up instead of a normal sit. It can be fixed with more clicker training.

From the beginning, you'll need to separate your trainee from the other cats, in order to teach it without interference. I do most of my individual training in the kitchen, with the door shut. Some people use the bathroom, as there are fewer distractions there. Wendy uses the staircase, sitting two steps below the cat. Going to the same place each time helps the cat zero in on what it's doing that makes you click. You may crate the cats you aren't working with, or shut them in another room. Don't worry that they'll hear the click and become confused; they can tell, by who's getting the treats, whether that click is important to them or not.

Once your cat has really learned a new skill, you may safely ask it to perform with the other cats around. Cats can learn by observation. Teach one cat to sit on a stool, or to ring a bell to get you to open a door, and the other cats may learn without individual shaping. All you need to do is to click and treat them, too, when they show signs of picking up the new behavior. It's a shortcut dolphin trainers use all the time.

Like dolphins, cats may learn the new behavior by watching, but they are unlikely to learn the cue spontaneously. You can handle this two ways: teach your primary animal the cue—go through the tunnel when I say "tunnel," for instance—and then reward any other cat that follows the first one's lead, or let them all discover how to do the behavior and then teach them its cue individually.

I usually have clicker sessions with one animal at a time if we're doing something new, but if it's something they all know, I may ask for the behavior ("Down" works for both my dogs and the cat at the same time) and then click once and toss treats to everybody. Visitors are always surprised when all your cats respond to a cue simultaneously, but learning by imitating each other is quite natural to cats—the phrase "copy cat" is no accident.

Fun Stuff

The clicker cat

What else can your clicker cat learn to do? Clicker trainer Wendy Jeffries maintains an e-mail list on the Internet for people who are clicker training cats (see Chapter Five, "Resources"). Behaviors that people on the list have taught their cats to do include spinning in place, "High five" (hold up paw and touch or slap your hand), "Sit pretty" (sit up with paws in the air), "Find your mat and lie on it" (a mouse pad, of course), "Stay" (especially useful to keep the cat from running out an open door), "Down," retrieving a ball, jumping hurdles, opening a cupboard door (by hooking a paw around it), closing a door or a drawer (by pushing it with both paws), and "Roll over." And, of course, the behaviors described in Chapters One and Two.

Cats love exercising their superb mobility, speed, and control. One owner tacked a strip of carpet to the wall and taught her cat to run up it to the ceiling, and then to come down backwards. Pat Brewington, a horse trainer who uses clicker techniques, taught one of her cats to make an impressive leap to the top of the refrigerator on cue. Another learned to reach into a small jar on the kitchen table and fish around with one paw like someone looking for car keys in a purse—a sight that for some reason invariably makes guests laugh hysterically. (Some people just can't stop clicking once they get started; Pat also used a grain reward to teach three mice in her barn to run around in circles on top of a barrel.)

Clicker cats can do most of the things dogs can do. Seattle police officer Steve White, a pioneer in the clicker training of search and detection dogs, trained his cat to track a person by scent, just like a K9 German shepherd on patrol. "Not much of a track," he said. "Only 150 feet; but up to that distance, he can definitely find the bad guy." (Steve confesses that in the early stages he spiked the human trail scent with just a touch of tuna.)

Cat agility

The new and popular sport of agility training for dogs, involving the running of obstacle courses, is perfectly suited to cats, who can easily learn to climb up and down a steep A-frame, run through tunnels, jump a series of hurdles, and weave in and out of a row of poles. You can set up obstacles around the house—under this chair, over that hassock, in and out of the wastebasket—and click the cat for a fast gallop over the course following your target stick. Catherine Crawmer, of *American Animal Trainer* magazine, is featured on my *Clicker Magic* video taking her cat over an entire agility course in just a few seconds. On that tape she also walks us through the beginning steps for each part of the training, including shaping the cat to go into a toy house (first opening the door with a paw) and then running out of the house through a flattened cloth tunnel. It's an instructive sight. The cat's curiosity, intelligence, and enthusiasm are very visible, even on camera.

Jan-Erik Andersson, a professional dog trainer in Sweden, acquired two kittens and decided to clicker train both of them. Working with one kitten at a time, he trained them to locate and lie down on a mouse pad anywhere in his apartment (using a video camera and TV monitor to watch the kitten from another room and click at the appropriate moment). Using just four or five clicks and treats per session, he also taught each of the kittens to jump over hurdles and go through tubes.

When his kittens were five months old, Jan-Erik decided to show off their clicker-trained agility behaviors at one of his dog training workshops. As reported on the Internet, in a strange place, in a room filled with dog owners and dogs (all, no doubt, equally astonished), both kittens performed their behaviors flawlessly.

Cat music

It's easy to teach a cat to play the piano; I've often done it in other people's houses, with their cat, as a sort of after-dinner amusement. First you lure the cat onto the piano bench with food, clicking as it jumps up. (Present the treats on a plate on the bench, so you don't get grease or tuna juice on your hostess's furniture.) Then you lure or target the cat forward until it puts a paw on the keys. *Click.* Repeat the process, fading the lure, until the cat is voluntarily stepping on the keys and looking at you for a click. Then begin reinforcing firmer touches until you get good noise-making hits (this is easier with an electronic keyboard than with a regular piano, but either will do).

Professor Jesus Rosales-Ruiz, who teaches in the Department of Behavior Analysis at the University of North Texas, requires all his students, both graduate and undergraduate, to clicker train a pet or some other animal. One of his students trained her cat not only to "play" the piano, but to strike one specific note. Then she put the behavior on a verbal cue. Ultimately she accomplished her rather ambitious goal. She sat at the piano and played part of a Mozart piece in G, while the cat sat next to her, waiting like an orchestra musician for its cue to come in. At the end she gave the cue "Play G," and the cat brought the piece to a close with a resounding plonk on the final signature note. *Click!* The student's A-grade term project consisted of a video showing the shaping process (including the things that did *not* work)—as well as the final successful performance.

Here's a further refinement on piano playing. Teach the cat to play the keys two or three times for a click. (This builds up endurance, so the cat won't quit just because it didn't get clicked for any one plonk; thus you have room to select and click only the right sort of plonks.) Put a removable sticker on Middle C, as a target, and click the behavior of playing that key only. (You might want to teach "aim for the sticker" separately, by clicking the cat for pawing stickers in other places before adding the task of recognizing the sticker to the piano-playing task.)

When the cat is hitting the marked key reliably, put another sticker just to the right, on D. Your aim is to establish the behavior of hitting D and then C for a click. You'll always be ending up on the note the cat first learned, C, so the cat can proceed with confidence. When D-C is accomplished, add the next note to the right, E, then shape the behavior of playing all three notes, right to left, one time each. Repeat. Presto! Your cat plays the first two bars of "Three Blind Mice."

Follow the dot: The ultimate cat sport

Pet stores sell lots of interactive cat toys you can use to amuse your cat: feathers on springs, battery-operated mice, and so on. One of the best toys in the world, for most cats, is the laser pointer, which you can get from any office supply store. Most cats will chase the sharp little red dot of light that the pointer makes right from the moment they see it. You can send the cat in any direction, at any speed. You can use the dot as a target to train other behavior, or you can use a bit of dot play as a reward for a good training session, as dog owners sometimes use ball play to reward good work.

Two words of caution. First, while modern laser pointers are not supposed to be harmful to the eyes, you shouldn't shine it at your cat's face—or anyone else's—but always a foot or so ahead of the cat. And don't let young children play with the pointer, for the same reason.

Here's the second warning: I haven't heard of a cat falling for this, but some dogs become so addicted to the laser dot that they can think of nothing else. An otherwise normal Rottweiler, for example, may take to stalking through the house hour after hour, panting, glassy-eyed, swinging his head, scanning the floor, looking for The Dot. Perhaps the dog's owner can ignore this, but sooner or later a roommate or spouse says, "I can't stand this loony dog another minute. Will you please make him stop?" The owner whips out the laser and gives the dog a game of chase-the-dot until it's so exhausted it has to sleep for a while. This placates the complainer, but also guarantees that the dog will search even longer and harder the next time.

Clicker trainer and teacher Sherri Lippman introduced me to the solution for this particular problem: always start and end the dot from the same place. Sherri uses the toe of her shoe. The dot first appears there, and then, when the game is over, goes back to disappear at the same spot. This helps the animal understands that the dot has gone for now and the worst that can happen is that for a time it might stare longingly at the toe of your shoe.

Although a simple verbal cue, used consistently, would also serve to begin and end this game, I like using a visual cue as well. Mine for Mimi, who loves the dot, is to put my hand in front of her and seemingly spill the dot out of my hand to start the game; then when I want to end it I slide the dot onto my hand again, close my fist as I turn the pointer off, and "take the dot away."

Naming behaviors: How to add a cue

How do you tell the cat which behavior, of the many things it can do for a click, you want it to do at this particular moment? When you know the behavior is going to happen, you introduce a cue: a word, a hand motion, or both. You click the cat for doing the behavior during or right after the cue, and by and by that signal becomes the tip-off to the cat that right now it will get clicked for that particular behavior.

Let's take rolling over as an example. If you've clicked rolling, you're going to see more of it. At first it seems like an accident: Oh, the cat's rolling again—where's my clicker? Then it becomes obvious that the behavior is increasing. The cat rolls several times a day, then the cat seems to be rolling on purpose. It occurs to the cat to do a bit of person training, so it runs ahead of you, flings itself down in front of you, and rolls over. The cat, in the words of clicker trainer Gary Wilkes, is "throwing the behavior at you."

Now the opportunity is ripe to teach the cat that there's a time when rolling will pay off and that at all other times it's a waste of effort. Think up a signal—a word or a gesture—to be your new cue for rolling. Gestures or body motions seem to be easier for cats (and dogs) to notice and identify than spoken words. You might want to start with a visible hand signal and then add a word cue later.

Give the signal as the cat starts to roll; then click and treat. (Be generous with clicks and treats while you're establishing a new cue; don't try to improve or refine the behavior at the same time. When the cue is clear to the cat, the behavior will improve by itself.) Gradually back the signal off until you are giving it before the roll occurs, and the cat is responding with the roll. You can then gradually stop reinforcing rollovers that occur when you didn't give a cue.

Cats seem to pick up cues very rapidly. (In fact, you may find that your cat responds to many of your own behaviors that you didn't intend as cues.) Once you see that the cat is doing the right behavior for your signal (sitting, say, when you hold your hand over its head), you might want to add some changes to the circumstances, to make the cue stronger. Try it when you're sitting down and then when you're standing, or in different parts of the room or in different rooms. Always click and treat the correct response. Try it when the cat isn't expecting it, or in distracting circumstances, such as when strangers are present. Every cue response you succeed in reinforcing in a new circumstance will strengthen the communicative bond between you and your clicker cat.

Multiple behaviors

What if you are trying to teach the cat one thing, to follow the target over a jump, say, and it does something else that you'd like to see again? Go ahead and click for the new behavior too. Won't it confuse the cat to be clicked for different behaviors? Not really. Each click builds a little more strength into that particular response, without weakening other, unrelated responses. Of course the cat may stop the targeting work you were doing and start offering the new behavior instead. That's fine. A dolphin might do exactly the same thing when learning something new. Switch over to clicking the new behavior. You can always go back to targeting later.

How many things can you work on in one training session? Julie Shaw, clicker training instructor at the Animal Behavior Clinic at Purdue University, wrote me, "I worked with our one-year-old kitten last night and had her targeting, giving me high-fives, spinning in a circle, and ALMOST sitting." That's in *one* training session, and it was the first real clicker session for this young cat.

While there isn't much data on this yet, it's beginning to look as if cats learn more easily if they are *not* asked to repeat a behavior over and over in a session, but instead clicked just a few times each for a variety of old and new behaviors. My dogs, when they're learning a new behavior, will gladly do it over and over and over, a hundred times or more, for clicks and treats. But doing the same thing over and over even a dozen times seems to be difficult for cats.

For example, when I was trying to teach Mimi to ring a bell, she would touch it with paw or nose for one or two clicks, but then she would walk away and offer some other behavior. I wanted to work on that one thing until some progress had been made, but she rarely concurred. My training log from that period shows that in one session Mimi earned twelve clicks for seven different behaviors in three minutes, but only two of those clicks involved the bell. Nevertheless, over the next two weeks, bell ringing did become stronger. She was actually patting the bell, finally, and my notes showed that her unclicked bell behaviors, namely smelling the bell and playing with the string it hangs from, were diminishing.

So, what the heck. In the immortal words of behaviorist Robert Bailey, rule number one is "Get the behavior, get the behavior, get the behavior." Nothing in science suggests that it's better—or worse—to get the behavior by reinforcing it twenty times in one day than by reinforcing it once a day for twenty days. We are following the cats in this matter.

High speed behavior

Some dog agility competitors have put forth a theory that slow, careful behavior, such as sitting or lying in one place, is best trained by giving a food reward, while high-speed behavior, such as zooming through a tunnel or over a series of jumps against the clock, is best trained by using a ball, frisbee, or other fast-moving toy as the reinforcer.

Is this true? With dolphins, and with my own dogs, I had been able to increase the speed of response by simply clicking prompt responses and turning away briefly if the response was slow, then giving the cue again. Gradually tightening the screws about how fast you have to respond to get clicked also tended to increase the speed of the behavior itself. The groups of dolphins I have trained responded to their cues in unison and within less than a second, and the leaps, racing, and spins they did were executed very rapidly as well.

With Mimi, since I'm usually limited to ten or twenty food treats a day, selecting for gradual increases in speediness might take ages. Would some kind of fast-moving reinforcer produce rapid behavior more easily? I had a chance to test the premise when Alexandra Kurland, author of *Clicker Training for*

Your Horse, sent Mimi a toy called the Cat Dancer, a piece of spring steel wire with a wooden gizmo on the end that leaps and wiggles. If I dangled and bounced the toy she would play violently until totally winded. I wanted to try using it as a reinforcer, instead of food. I asked Mimi to sit up, she did, I clicked and then offered the toy instead of chicken. Mimi was THRILLED.

She would do anything for the Cat Dancer. One drawback: she decided to do nothing without it.

The next morning I asked for Mimi some normal behavior. I think it was "Close the drawer." She did the behavior; I clicked and tossed a treat. Whereupon Mimi ignored the treat and stared at me. "Yes, I will do any behavior you like, but I want that TOY, not food, for pay." I would not produce the toy. Mimi stopped eating almost entirely for three days. On the third day I offered her pieces of fresh, warm, sauteed breast of chicken, her most prized food. She not only wouldn't eat it, she tried to bury it. "I spit on your gifts."

Finally, on the fourth day, Mimi showed an interest in her kitchen tricks and treats again. We did her usual behaviors at her chosen and rather methodical pace, for the usual treats, which Mimi now ate without any display of disdain. Then, while Mimi watched, I got the Cat Dancer out of the drawer where it is kept. She quivered with excitement. I held it behind me and tapped my finger on the back of the couch as a target. Wham! Mimi was there in one incredibly fast eight-foot jump from the floor, nose to my finger. *Click!* And she earned a ten-second Cat Dancer session.

We had struck a bargain. She would do her regular tricks and learn new ones for a click and a treat, pleasantly but not especially quickly. She will do her new, high-speed racing and leaping behaviors, zooming up walls and across obstacles like a motocross rider wherever I target her to go, for the Cat Dancer. She has offered me the instant takeoff and extremely rapid performance right from the very first trial without any sign of slackening speed.

Both the high-speed targeting and the incredible maneuvers she executes with this toy in play are exhausting. Mimi can only do the combination three or four times in a row before she flops panting to the floor. However, she targets to my finger at top speed every evening, given the chance, and will gladly exhibit her on-cue Cat Thrillarama behaviors for guests.

I asked Catherine Crawmer, who has trained zoo lions and tigers as well as house cats, whether she thought chase-rewards were valuable, or maybe even necessary, for high-speed behavior. Catherine considered it a given, at least for cats, for biological reasons. "Take tigers, for instance. You may think your cat sleeps a lot. Tigers sleep twenty-three out of twenty-four hours a day. Never mind how interesting the environment is, or how nice the company. One big burst of effort is all they've got, and that better get them dinner. Otherwise they move slowly. So if you want a tiger to jump fast, food isn't in it; you use the little tassel on the end of a lunge whip, as a toy, to get them to pounce to the next stool. That's the way to trigger real energy expenditure."

Clicker training and communication

Cats have many ways of indicating that they want something. Kittens mew when they need their mothers; most older cats spontaneously meow when they want assistance, for example, to have a door opened; and once a cat of my acquaintance virtually yelled for help when she'd cornered a rat that was too big to kill alone. I have seen a clicker-trained tiger, in a zoo, look disconsolately at a toy that had floated away in its pond, and then turn its great face to the keeper and say, plaintively, "Mew?" as in "You get it for me, okay?"

In addition to whatever tools nature gives them, cats quickly learn to use their newly acquired clicker skills to communicate. Once some years ago, while visiting my cousin and his wife, I trained their cat to play the piano. That is, I used bits of ham to shape the behavior of sitting on the bench and hitting the keys with one paw. I went home and no one ever asked the cat to play the piano again, nor did it try to do so.

Two years later my cousin called to tell me that the night before, after they had gone to bed, they were wakened by ghostly sounds of someone downstairs in the living room playing the piano. They went to investigate, opened the living room door, and found the cat sitting on the piano bench, plinking on the keys. Normally this cat slept upstairs in the bedroom. It had accidentally been shut in the living room and left behind. One presumes that when the normal responses of meowing and perhaps scratching at the door didn't work, the cat offered a behavior it had learned two years previously to ask, not for food this time, but for its preferred sleeping place—and the effort was rewarded.

Learning to learn; a benefit of clicker training

No matter what species you are clicker training—dogs, cats, horses, goldfish, giraffes—the process itself has a wonderful benefit: the animals don't just learn the behavior you are reinforcing; they *learn to learn*. Cats that have acquired a lot of clicked behaviors become—well, I don't want to say they become more intelligent; but I think it would be fair to say they learn to use their capabilities more fully. You have given them a much richer environment, through the clicker cat games, so they can make better use of the resources they do have, and they can sometimes communicate and interact with you in downright creative ways.

Tosca, the New York Burmese, spent a lot of time devising ways to circumnavigate the New York apartment on the tops of the furniture without having to get down on the floor. The living room, lined with bookcases, was easy. My daughter Gale's bedroom was a challenge. Tosca could go from the desk to the table to the bed, and then to the top of the bookcase—that took her around three walls of the room. But getting from the bookcase back to the desk meant crossing two doorways, one to the living room and one to the closet. It was too wide a gap to jump.

Have you ever seen your cat sit and study an access problem? "How am I going to accomplish this?" Tosca must have spent some time on this issue. One day I heard her yowling vigorously. "Come here. Come here now!" So I went. Tosca was in Gale's room. She was standing on the two-inch-wide top of the open door to the living room. "Tosca, how did you get up there!" I exclaimed, but I could see that she must have jumped from the bookcase.

Now that she had my attention, with an easy spring Tosca leapt from the top edge of the living room door to the top edge of the closet door three feet away. Neither door moved an inch as she did this. She landed as she had taken off, with all four feet in a line.

What a feat! It required her to go straight up from the first door (so as not to push it laterally and throw off her aim) and then to come straight down onto the second, so as not to push it sideways and spill her onto the floor. And from platforms almost too narrow even for a cat.

"Tosca, that's perfectly AMAZING. What a wonderful CAT you are," I said. Tosca sat carefully down on the door and burst into a purr you could have heard in Brooklyn.

Tosca was showing me something she had learned on her own. I suspect that the clarity and variety of our interactions had developed a circumstance in which she was inclined to experiment and learn, and a circumstance in which she was also inclined to share and communicate with me.

The confidence and communicative skills of a clicker cat are not limited to interactions with its owner. Tosca captivated many people in her lifetime. My present clicker cat, Mimi, is so forthright in her human encounters, and so confident of a response back, that several one-time guests to the house have been smitten to the point of getting themselves a new cat of the same breed. Admittedly the Burmese breed has a reputation for sociability, but it seems to me that the learning skills developed through clicker transactions can make any cat's social skills bloom.

Rich repertoires and richer relationships

Graduate student Scott McKenzie, challenged by his University of North Texas clicker training course requirements, decided to train his cat, Puck, to turn out the bedroom light. It was easy to get the cat to touch the light switch, but difficult to develop a push sufficient to turn it off or on. Scott's solution was to shape the behavior of stepping on a big, brightly colored paper circle on the floor. Once the cat was good at that, Scott moved the disk around, made it smaller, clicked for harder touches, and then moved it to the wall. Soon Puck would swat it, even on the wall. Scott rewired the switch with a push-plate instead of a standard protruding switch; he made the plate as sensitive as possible, and then taped it so it was almost but not quite switched. He then faded the target disc to coin size and moved it to the switch, which the cat could reach from the back of the couch. Finally the behavior was complete. I have seen it on video. On the cue, "Puck! Light off," the cat leaps from floor to couch and swats the switch to turn out the light and plunges the room into darkness.

The final step, of course, was for Scott to back away from the switch until he could cue the cat from a distance; thus, with the help of his assistant, he could turn out the lights without getting out of bed.

In addition to this highly useful behavior, Puck has learned to knock pool balls into the pocket from any place on the table—often from a considerable distance and into any indicated pocket. The training steps were tap a rolling ball, tap a still ball, tap a still ball balanced right next to the hole until it falls in, tap from further away, until skills develop to aim the ball, and finally, tap the ball to the pocket Scott is pointing to.

Puck now has some forty behaviors in her repertoire. "When I'm driving home from school," Scott told me, "I'm thinking about what I'm going to teach her today." Scott's professor, Dr. Rosales-Ruiz, tells his students that a behavior should be trained to the point where it can happen anywhere, with anything going on. Scott habituated Puck to going friends' houses in the cat carrier. "Not to parties, of course, but five or six people is okay. I shaped it up, I trained...in all different rooms. I just have to warn the people not to play with the clicker—it means too much to her."

In fact, Puck and Scott mean a lot to each other. Training sessions are a highlight of the day. "Pick up the clicker and she just goes nuts," Scott says. "It has definitely drawn us closer. It's an experience we can share, that we both love to do. People don't realize how much fun it is, and how dramatically it changes the relationship, for you and for the animals too."

Scott MacKenzie's professional work is with children with developmental disabilities. Honing his shaping skills with Puck has been an illuminating experience that he has applied to his work with children:

> You have to be systematic, you have to be on time with your reinforcers. You have to know when to put down the clicker, while you step back and look at the rules of shaping. It's never the learner's fault, it's always in the teaching. What am I doing wrong here?
>
> You have to see the one tiny next step. People who only look for big changes can't make progress. And the result, the wonderful reinforcing bond that you build between you through successful shaping experiences, comes in just the same way with people with developmental disorders.

Not just for house cats

Clicker training is being used more and more widely in animal care in zoos, where it's often referred to as husbandry training. In the old days, big dangerous animals like lions and tigers were moved from one area to another by baiting, and if that didn't work, by force (prods or fire hoses, for example). Nowadays, moving big predators from one area to another is often accomplished by targeting. And any physical care the animal might need, from protective vaccinations to inspection and treatment of a wound, can be facilitated with clicks and treats. One keeper asks the lion, say, to hold his nose to a target against the cage bars, while another gently draws a routine blood sample from the lion's tail. Clicker training makes handling and medical care easier and safer, while the mental exercise and social experience is stimulating and enriching for the animals.

Cats in animal shelters also benefit from clicker training. Standing outside the cage with a clicker, a spoon, and a can of cat food, one can teach a shy cat to come forward, a standoffish cat to make eye contact and maybe even purr, and a bold, pushy cat to back up or to sit for a treat. In some shelters volunteers are clicker training the cats, including abandoned and feral animals, providing enrichment in a difficult environment, and also, in some cases, making a cat more adoptable. Looking for new challenges, besides working with your own pet? Take your clicker and volunteer at your nearest animal shelter. The dogs, cats, and staff will all be delighted to see you.

Problems and Solutions

Some cat problems are physical—illness, infections, parasites, injury—and these are the province of your veterinarian. Behavior problems are less easily dealt with, and most veterinarians are not trained as behavior specialists.

Often clicker training can help. Some behavior can be specifically retrained with the clicker. If a cat is misbehaving out of boredom, or because misbehaving is the only way to get attention, just establishing a program of positive reinforcement can make a huge difference, no matter what you train the cat to do. Some behavioral problems, however, are not really training problems, but are due to some aspect of the environment. The commonest problem of this sort is failure to use the litterbox.

Litterbox problems

One of the things that makes cats such great pets is that they can almost always can be relied on to relieve themselves outdoors or in the indoor place provided on their own, without our direct involvement. In fact they are *so* reliable that we get frantic when the system breaks down. Cat waste smells terrible; it's not something one can put up with for long. The absolute number one reason people give an otherwise delightful cat up for adoption is that the cat is eliminating in the wrong places.

A common cause of avoiding the litter box is urinary tract infections, to which cats are very prone. An infection can make urinating painful. The cat may blame it on the box and try to find a more comfortable place to go. Take any cat whose behavior changes in this regard to the vet; treatment may include medication and a diet change.

Another cause of spraying and urinating outside the box is territorial marking. New cats, not just in the house but in the neighborhood, may provoke territorial marking, even in an indoor cat. And if a previous outdoor cat seems afraid to leave the house, think about rival cats lurking outside. Talk to your vet, do some reading (see Chapter Five, "Resources"), or find an animal behaviorist to consult.

Often, however, the problem is caused not by the cat but by its owner:

The litter box is too dirty to use.

Litter should be scooped daily and changed often. The pan itself needs to be clean: empty and scrub it now and then. A cat may put up with a soiled litter box for a long time and then suddenly reach its limit of tolerance and look for some better spot. If no one in the household is willing to do daily maintenance, invest in one of the automatic self-cleaning litterbox systems (see Chapter Five, "Resources"). They are expensive, but worth it (you'll still need to clean it thoroughly from time to time). A veterinarian I know, with a family and two cats, firmly maintains that the self-cleaning litter box saved his marriage.

The litter box is not easy to get to.

Veterinarian behaviorist Andy Lattal told me he solved one litter box crisis over the phone. He asked the client where she kept the box. In the hall closet, she said. Could the cat get into the closet easily? Well, actually sometimes the door was closed. Why was the door closed? Well, in order to open the cellar door, you had to close the closet door, and sometimes after she came up from the cellar she forgot to open the closet again. Dr. Lattal's solution: Take the door off the closet and put it in the cellar. A few days later the client called, thrilled: the cat was completely clean again. "I thought you had to be a Hollywood trainer," she said, "to work such miracles."

There are too many cats using the same box.

Cats have complex social relationships, just like people. Some cats hate sharing a litter box. Others get along fine for a while and then decide they can't share. A new cat added to the household, or a kitten reaching maturity, may tip the balance. It's not unheard of to have one litter box for each cat. Put more boxes in more places, and keep them all clean. Cats should not have to compete for litter time, or be afraid of being pounced on or threatened in a private moment.

No matter what the cause of elimination outside the litter box, stopping the problem takes some effort and attention. Management may include confining the cat to a crate at times, medication, a change of diet, removing some other specific cat from the household, removing or disinfecting anything the cat has soiled, and more. Here's one place where neither punishment nor positive reinforcers can make much difference. The cat hasn't "forgotten" where to go, and it's doing its best to meet its own needs and stay clean. You have to find out what's getting in the way of that process.

"Aggression" toward humans

I've put the word "aggression" in quotes because I think it is both overused and misused. What one person calls aggression another might see as normal play or justifiable self-protection. If your cat is biting or scratching enough to upset you, ask yourself first if anything you are doing is actually reinforcing that. Does the cat get some desirable result? Can it chase you away from your own couch, or make you stop petting it when it wants to be left alone, with this misbehavior? Or are you trying to be so nice to the cat that you are encouraging it to get pricklier in your normal interactions? You can change your behavior so you don't reward roughness inadvertently, and you can use the clicker to teach gentleness (See Chapter Two, under "Gentle Paws").

Sometimes aggression—hissing, spitting, swatting—is the result of mistreatment or abuse at the hands of a human. More often it is a manifestation of lack of experience and socialization. Many people spend a lot of time teaching their dogs to be comfortable around strangers and visitors; but we seldom bother to socialize our cats. Do you introduce your cat to new people who come to the house? Most likely not, but you could. Use your clicker to teach the cat that new people are good for clicks and treats.

The clicker is also an enormously useful tool for socializing feral cats and kittens or animals that have been neglected or abandoned. You can click any step in your direction, or any sign of confidence, and then toss the food to the cat, or drop it in a bowl that you will leave behind you when you go. Cats quickly learn to try to make you click, even if they don't actually eat the food until later.

Ankle-biting

Healthy young cats love to attack moving objects, and as a kitten reaches adolescence, that may well include you. The cat tackles your feet under the table, or hides under the furniture and ambushes you as you pass with energetic use of teeth and claws. The cure is to make it less fun. If you freeze and don't move the very first time this happens, the cat may give up on the spot.

Ankle-biting is almost always a sign that the cat is feeling her new growth and strength, and craves action. Of course clicker training in itself is a great help for a cat that is restless and looking for activity. The more behaviors you train, the more the cat has to think about and do; less desirable activities, such as ambushing, will tend to fade away by themselves.

If you want to intervene directly, get some action toys, such as feathers on a spring, or even just a piece of aluminum foil on the end of a string. Use the toy to give the cat a satisfying chase-and-play session once or twice a day. This may satisfy the need to stalk and pounce, and you can incorporate the toy into your clicker training sessions, often with great results (see Chapter Three, under "High speed behavior"). If the cat still stalks your feet, try the solution offered by one cat owner: Wear boots indoors, so you don't care if the cat attacks your ankles or not, until the cat outgrows the urge.

The leopard leap: Ambushes from above

At about the age of two, the arboreal Burmese, Tosca, developed the habit of hiding on the top of a bookcase and dropping unexpectedly onto the shoulder of a person walking past beneath her. It was always a surprise to me, and for visitors, especially cat-fearing visitors, it was an appalling shock.

Since this behavior was increasing, I knew somehow it was being reinforced. What did Tosca like about it? Maybe, I thought, she liked riding around on someone's shoulder. So whenever I happened to see her sitting in a semi-high place, on a windowsill, say, I began holding out my hands and offering to pick her up. Tosca was then apt to sit up on her haunches, paws in the air, to facilitate being lifted. If she did that, I "clicked" her with a praise word, picked her up as a reward, and carried her around for a little while on my shoulder, giving her a view of such exciting unfamiliar scenes as the inside of the medicine cabinet and the top shelf of the closet.

Tosca now had a very specific way to communicate her wishes. If she felt like having a ride, she watched where I was walking, ran ahead of me, jumped onto a counter or window sill, and sat up, paws in the air, as I went by: "Taxi!" I almost always obliged, and the leopard attacks stopped.

Scratching and ripping upholstery

The scratch marks cats make on furniture are not done to sharpen their nails, but to mark their territory. The scratches call attention to the spot, which carries the cat's scent and also indicates the height and strength of the cat that made the marks. A scratched-up area is a signpost designed to tell other cats that this terrain belongs to *your* cat.

Some cats put more effort into their territorial markers than other cats do, but most cats like a good scratching place; even de-clawed cats go through the motions. Cats like to choose a spot that's conspicuous, and are particularly attracted to something new in the environment (such as the most visible side of your new couch). The best way to prevent furniture destruction is to preempt the site selection process by providing an ideal site that the cat is allowed to mark up.

What makes a good scratching place? It should be vertical and very solid, so the cat can really use all its muscles without the thing wobbling or falling over (a fatal flaw of some commercial scratching posts). It should have the right kind of surface, deep enough for claws to sink in, but soft enough so that it shreds or seems to shred—the cat, after all, wants to leave a mark. Commercial posts that are wrapped with rope are better than those wrapped with carpet. Veterinarian behaviorist Nicholas Dodman suggests layers of burlap nailed to a panel and mounted on a wall or the side of a cupboard, or best of all, a real log with bark on it, screwed onto a platform so it can't tip over. Both of these objects shred delightfully (and thus will need to be resurfaced or replaced from time to time).

Some cats (but not all) will settle for a horizontal scratching place. You can make the new site more attractive by adding catnip, if your cat likes catnip. Of course you can also click and treat, first for sniffing the new place and then for actual scratching. Several clicker trainers report that they have successfully transferred the territorial signpost by providing a good sturdy substitute and then clicking for the new place and covering the old one with plastic temporarily.

Scratching in the wrong place is often accidentally reinforced. Recently, my son Mike and his wife Eileen bought a new couch. Naturally the cat started scratching it. Every time that happened, Mike grabbed the cat and put it outside. One night as he was reading the paper he noticed that the cat was sitting in the living room staring at him. As he watched, the cat strolled to the couch and prepared to scratch. He grabbed the cat—and then it dawned on him. After her dinner the cat liked to go outside. She had trained him to put her out on cue—her cue—scratching the couch. The next night, when the cat came into the living room and stared at him, Mike got up and let her out *before* she scratched. It did not eliminate scratching entirely, but at least it eliminated it as a method of cat-to-human communication.

Boredom

Many of the things cats do that annoy us are related to boredom. Licking, wool-sucking, pacing back and forth, self-grooming to the point of losing hair or creating a sore spot—these stereotypic or repetitive behaviors are all at least partially manifestations of insufficient stimulation in the environment. Digging in the houseplants, knocking things off the mantel, or unrolling the toilet paper are initially play activities, and are a natural part of exploration. It's only when they become repeated, persistent, flagrant behavior that intervention is called for. The first step is to watch yourself and see if you are paying attention to the cat only or mostly when it does that bad thing. Even yelling is attention and may serve to escalate the behavior. Then get out the clicker and give the cat some better things to do. Establishing a clicker routine and developing a daily bout of clicker fun with the cat is the fastest and easiest way to change the cat's life and consequently its bad behavior.

Yowling

Some breeds of cats are more vocal than others (Siamese, especially). Meowing and noisemaking can escalate to intolerable levels. Sometimes there may be medical reasons for agitation, and the help of a veterinary behaviorist can be invaluable, but often it's a question of what you are doing, not the cat. One new member of the cat clicker list complained that her cat vocalized so loudly it actually screamed. On the list's advice she tried just turning her back on her cat whenever it made a noise. Bingo. The noise dwindled away. She had been reinforcing the behavior, without knowing it.

Another newcomer to the clicker list complained that her cat never meowed at all, except occasionally when she gave it a bath. She wanted a chatty cat. Could she increase the cat's vocalizing by clicking? Many on the list were amused, but they said she could, and she did. She also, on their advice, added a Siamese cat to the household.

Jumping on table during meals

Some people don't mind if cats jump on the table while a meal is going on; I know one family that cheerfully allows its cat to wander around and help itself from people's plates. More often, owners try to scare the cat off, or lift it down, but never really get rid of the behavior. One reasonable solution is just to confine the cat elsewhere during meals, or at least during dinner parties with guests. Another way to avoid table surfing is to simply never let it happen, right from the beginning, so the cat knows that jumping on the table during meals is always futile: the people always put you down at once. If, however, the cat has been getting away with it now and then, you can intervene by training an incompatible behavior. Teach him to sit on a nearby stool or chair, where initially you can reinforce the behavior with occasional treats. Then extend the duration of the time the cat will wait, until he sits patiently throughout a meal (see Chapter Two, under "Places, please"). Once the behavior is complete, the treat can be given in the kitchen after the table is cleared.

Finicky eaters

Cats are famous for being finicky about their food. I've learned something new to me, watching Mimi growing up. Mimi is very careful about what goes in her body. She doesn't eat stale food. She's suspicious of new food, and may just smell it, or barely taste it, for a meal or two, before accepting it or not. I now suspect finicky eating isn't snootiness at all, but a necessary trait with a biological basis. Cats are *solitary obligate predators.* In the wild they must kill and eat all their food by themselves. What they eat, being what they've just killed, is always absolutely fresh. Dogs can kill big prey and then share the carcass with each other until it's all gone. They can bury bones and dig them up and enjoy them, rotten or not, days or weeks later. Cats can't do that.

Dogs don't mind dirty water. They will drink from a puddle in the street, from a goldfish pond or, famously, from the toilet. By the end of the day the animals' water bowl on the floor of my kitchen has all kinds of junk in it—sand, leaves, food—carried in on the dogs' muzzles. They don't care. Mimi does. It's her habit to have a long drink of water first thing in the morning and again before dinner, like a tiger coming down to a stream. If last night's water is still in the dog bowl in the morning, she tries a lap or two, and then leaves. If I empty the bowl, rinse out the canine debris, wipe the insides, and fill it with fresh water, she rushes back and has her long drink. I suspect cats have rather poor defenses against bacteria and other kinds of contamination. Drinking only clean water and eating only clean food is due not to arrogance but to evolution. They can't afford to do otherwise.

Being an obligate predator may also contribute to the feline tendency to choose one kind of food and eat nothing else. The same is true, I'm told by falconers, of young birds of prey (also solitary obligate predators). Whatever they first catch, on their first trial hunting flights, they specialize in from then on. Why risk a change, when what you're doing is working?

Some people simply give in to the cat's choice. A neighbor of mine kept a cat apparently healthy for its entire life on the only two things it would eat, chicken livers and cantaloupe. This approach can be pretty inconvenient, however—what if you ever run out of the Only Food, or need to change the cat's diet for health reasons? Varying the cat's diet, right from the beginning, even if it sometimes rejects your offerings at first, is a good idea, and it will facilitate your clicker training. You want the cat to begin looking forward to a variety of treats.

Shedding

If shedding is a real issue for you, because you have a longhaired cat or because someone in the house is allergic, here's a handy clicker solution: train your cat to enjoy being vacuumed. Is that possible? I've seen it done, and clicking makes it easy.

Choose the soft round furniture brush from the extension tools. Without attaching the brush to the vacuum hose, click and treat the cat for sitting still while you brush it with the new object. Then shape its tolerance for being touched by the brush while the tool is attached to the vacuum's handle and hose. The next step is clicking for tolerance to the noise. Put the vacuum in another room. Have someone else turn it on and off while you click and treat the cat each time the sound starts up. You may get away with this only once on the first day, but if you make it a part of the daily pre-supper routine the cat will adjust.

If you have no helper, put the vacuum cleaner as far away as possible and take the cat, the electric plug, and yourself into the bathroom. Then you can turn the machine on and off by plugging it in and pulling the plug out while clicking and treating with the other hand every time you turn it on. Once the cat discovers it is being paid for this sound, you can reintroduce the brush and hook it up. When the fear is gone, most cats seem to enjoy the funny feeling of being vacuumed, and you can significantly reduce the amount of hair and dander floating around the premises.

Getting stuck in trees

We have mostly been talking about indoor cats. If your cat is allowed outside, I recommend a little preventive training with regard to trees. Cats get stuck in trees because they don't know how to come down. Going up is easy. The cat is alarmed, it begins to run, and the design of its claws enables it to run straight up the trunk. Coming down is not so easy or automatic. The cat has to unhook its claws, one paw at a time, and reattach each paw further down, one by one, in order to back down the tree without falling off. It's a complicated process.

Perhaps kittens used to learn how to come down trees backwards by watching their mothers do it. But nowadays even if the kittens do get some outdoor time, we tend to take them away from their mothers before they are old enough for such adventures, so their first tree can become a real predicament. With a clicker, and gentle touch (rather than food), you can be the teacher. Here's how:

Before you let the cat run free outside, look around for a tree or post that is thick enough for a cat to climb—at least six inches around—with no low cross bars or branches. A phone pole will do in a pinch. Put the cat in a harness, let out about eight feet of leash, and tie the leash securely to your belt. You want the cat to be able to get high enough so that she's uneasy about just turning around and jumping down, but you want to be able to stop her if she bolts upwards.

Then pick the cat up and stick her on the tree or pole, as high up as you can comfortably reach. She's likely to grab on and freeze, looking down nervously. Now gently unhook one front paw, move it down an inch, hook it in again, click, and release. Do the same with the opposite hind leg. *Click.* Then move the other front paw, and then its opposite hind leg. Click when you feel any inclination in the cat's muscles to relax, or to slide a foot down by itself. Praise and stroking can be reassuring too, but the click gives the cat the vital information: "Oh, it's this paw movement that gets me out of here."

Once you've helped each of the four feet to move downward once or twice, the cat should be ready to creep and slide down the rest of the way by herself. Stand back and let her do so, however awkwardly. The cat will have the general idea, and you can leave practice and improvement to her.

Cat fights

Fighting arises most often when a new adult cat is introduced into a household that already contains one or more adult cats. Sometimes cats make friends easily, and sometimes not. Try letting them work it out themselves; with luck the hierarchy will soon be reshuffled successfully so that peace returns. Punishment of the attacker or the victim or both, perhaps by throwing things or spraying water, almost never works; it just makes the cats even madder at each other.

Sometimes it helps to provide crates or dens for each cat, elevated off the floor as cats prefer, so that the weaker cat has a cozy and defensible space of its own to retreat to when necessary. Cats can be initially accustomed to the crates by shutting them inside with toys, food, and catnip or by clicking them for exploring and going into the crates.

Many people have successfully used clicker training to teach enemy cats to tolerate each other. One begins by clicking and treating both cats for being in the same room at the same time. Then one clicks if the more aggressive cat looks away from the other—then for one or both cats sitting calmly in the same room, for getting nearer to each other without spitting and so on—until the cats can sit side by side, looking at the trainer instead of each other, for a click and a treat. This detox program may actually result in the cats becoming friends. "Oh, *she's* not so bad after all." Once affiliative behavior crops up—sniffing or licking each other, or mutual grooming—the job is done.

As always, check to see if you might be inadvertently reinforcing behavior you want to discourage. Once after a clicker training lecture I was approached by a psychologist who complained to me of an "aggression problem." His cats held pitched battles in the middle of the night, every night. It had started with just yowls but was now escalating to real injuries. Every night he "had to" get up to separate them, and calm them down by feeding them. Who was training whom?

Cats and dogs

Are you bringing a new cat in to live with an old dog? Or vice versa? This is not necessarily a disaster: cats and dogs can become very good friends.

First think about simple management matters. Each animal needs a private sleeping place. For the cat a back hall, a bathroom, an office, or even a closet can become night quarters, at least until diplomatic relations have been established. Provide a box or a shelf with some bedding in it, preferably elevated off the floor. Cats feel safer if they are not on the ground.

Next put up a couple of baby gates so that the new animal and the old animal can meet and see and smell each other through the barriers without actually coming in contact. Feed the animals separately, perhaps in separate rooms, at least at first. Make sure the cat has escape routes in case a chase erupts: physically show the cat or kitten places it can jump up to or crawl under, to get out of the way. If the dog is inclined to chase the cat you might let it drag a leash around the house for a couple of days, so you can step on the leash and stop any overly ambitious behavior. Don't let chases get out of hand; stop the dog if it goes after the cat and confine or tether it at once. Don't scold or punish—that won't help. Most of all, teach both animals the meaning of the clicker. Click and treat the dog copiously for being quiet while the cat is around, and for coming to you when you call it to interrupt a chase.

An older cat meeting a puppy can usually establish proper decorum with one edifying swat on the nose, and even kittens seem to be well wired for teaching dogs manners. I once introduced an eight-week-old kitten into a household that included a large male Weimaraner. The Weimaraner was polite enough to accept the edict that he couldn't take the kitten in his mouth, but instead he pointed at it—one front foot in the air, his nose six inches from the cat, and his entire body quivering—for two days. The kitten meanwhile went about its business of investigating the house, climbing in the bookcases, playing with bits of paper, and snoozing on the furniture. "Dog? What dog?"

The dog's behavior finally and abruptly extinguished, and he was calm and civil around the cat from then on.

Curing the cat-chasing dog: A clicker story

When I brought Mimi the Burmese home at the age of twelve weeks I was quite worried about my older dog. I felt sure that my young poodle, Misha, and the new kitten would rapidly become friends and playmates (which they did). However Twitchett, a nine-year-old border terrier, represented a serious threat. In fact, one senior animal behaviorist had e-mailed me advising that I rethink my plan of getting a kitten.

Twitchett, like all terriers, was bred to hunt small prey, and she was a fanatic. Where I used to live, in the mountains of the Pacific Northwest, Twitchett had pursued, caught, killed, and dragged into the house a wide variety of critters, from mice and rats to a half-grown opossum. As far as I know she never caught a cat, but she had been allowed and indeed encouraged to drive feral cats off the property, in order to protect the birds at my bird feeders. In her view, chasing cats, and killing them if possible, would be both a responsibility and a pleasure.

Twitchett knew, from both instinct and practice, how to grab and shake a small animal all in one motion, to break its spine. At least at first, one unguarded exposure of terrier to cat and this cherished (and expensive) kitten might be dead. Here's how I used the clicker to solve the problem.

I established the kitten in my home office with the door closed. Until further notice I would play with and clicker train the kitten only in the office or the kitchen. I kept Twitchett in another part of the house, also behind closed doors.

On the first evening I shut Twitchett up in a sturdy airline shipping crate in the kitchen and put Misha, the gentlemanly poodle, on a leash. The cat was released to investigate them. Misha responded to the kitten's approaches with dog-to-dog social behavior: sniffing, licking, tail wagging, and giving the calming signals of a lowered or averted head if the cat glared at him. Perfect. Twitchett, meanwhile, howled, yapped, and scratched at the crate door continuously, especially when the kitten (of course) jumped up onto the crate and peered insolently through the air holes. I let this go on for fifteen minutes, then put the cat back in the office with her dinner and released the dogs and fed them.

On the second evening of close encounters in the kitchen, Misha was allowed to play with the cat, with his leash trailing and me hovering behind to step on it if a chase got too rough. Twitchett, watching from the crate, continuously howled and tried to get out. "That's a cat. Let me out, I can get rid of it for you!"

I clicked and treated Twitchett for any brief moments of silence. I also fed treats to the cat with each click, to maintain her clicker conditioning. After five or ten minutes of this I put the cat back in the office and released the dogs into the living room, using a baby gate in the hall between the rooms to prevent Twitchett from snuffing, crying, and scratching at the office door all night as she was undoubtedly planning to do.

For the next few nights, while the evening news was running on the TV, I tethered both dogs to heavy furniture in the living room, supplied myself with clickers and treats, and let the kitten in (she was dying of curiosity and anxious to join us). The kitten could go where she wanted, and soon she and Misha began learning how to play together. Meanwhile I clicked Twitchett for looking away from the cat, however briefly, then for relaxing into a sit (uncued by me), then for relaxing further and lying down, and then for lying down and watching me.

I started using a verbal marker for Twitchett, the word "Good," which she knew meant "click" but the others didn't. Gradually Twitchett began regarding these evening social sessions not as a thwarted opportunity to chase cats, but as an opportunity to be clicked and treated. Her focus shifted from panting quivering attention on the kitten, to yearning wide-eyed attention on me. "Will I get clicked? How can I persuade her of my need for more food?"

By the time we'd done this nightly for a week or so, the kitten began to take what I considered terrible chances. Once when Twitchett was standing still, hoping for a click, the kitten dashed right through her legs and vanished under the couch, moving so fast that Twitchett could only stare. Then she took to batting Twitchett's whiskers and tail (click, treat) and then to rolling on her back and letting Twitchett lick and nibble her belly fur. I was nervous, but it was the cat's initiative, so I let it happen. As a precaution, I kept the tethered Twitchett right next to me and also held her firmly by the collar, and I put the kitten away at once if the terrier began whining or showing increased excitement. Mimi ended these sessions sopping wet, but she didn't seem to mind. Twitchett ended them with a click and a big treat.

Mimi had been with us about three weeks when she completed Twitchett's cure. Twitchett, tethered as usual, was lying next to me and quietly enjoying a new bone when Mimi jumped off the couch and landed on her back. Twitchett didn't even turn her head—she just picked up her bone and moved away.

I knew that the worst was over. Twitchett had just treated the kitten as a sort of puppy, as a juvenile social acquaintance rather than prey. "Don't bother me now, kid. I'm busy." From then on I could begin allowing Twitchett off the leash for brief periods of social play with the cat. As Mimi ferociously attacked Twitchett's front leg, or left ear, or wagging tail, the dog just looked at me: "Do I get clicked for this?" Yes indeed.

Mimi then began to initiate chases with Twitchett, bouncing sidewise and then bolting away right under her nose. A risky sport, I thought, but the cat had a plan. Just when Twitchett was about to catch her, she disappeared. Then, while the dog stood still, looking around in confusion ("Where'd she go? She was right here, I almost had her!") from some nearby shelf or table the cat would drop onto Twitchett's back.

Twitchett just *hated* this. The look of confusion and embarrassment on her face was priceless. Finally she would respond to a chase invitation, run three or four steps, and then stop, sigh ("I know where this is going"), and grumpily come back to the couch and lie down. Dogs play checkers, but cats play chess.

Until Mimi was about six months old I kept her shut safely away from Twitchett whenever I wasn't home, in case the two dogs chased the cat together and things got out of hand, but finally even that precaution became unnecessary. Twitchett now treats Mimi like a beloved child. She washes Mimi's face every morning, takes naps curled up with her on the couch, and lets her steal her toys. All three animals greet guests at the door. We are a family.

Does this all seem like a lot of trouble? It really wasn't. It took me ten or twenty minutes a night, while I was watching the news anyway. As long as we were making progress, I knew we would reach the goal of complete peace, and we did. Was it worth it? You bet! Otherwise I couldn't have a cat, and everyone needs a cat.

Clicker training as communication

Mimi is now a nearly year old. She doesn't have a huge trained repertoire; she knows a few cute tricks. More importantly to me, she knows a whole bunch of appropriate ways to tell me what's on her mind. Although Burmese cats are said to be pretty vocal, Mimi never meows (unless she gets shut in the hall closet). Why should she? She can get my attention at once by making eye contact ("Yes, Mimi? You wanted something?"). She can ask for food by sitting on a chair. She can ask for toys by patting the toy drawer. She can ask to go through doors by standing and pushing on them. She can ask for the company of the dogs by running toward the room they are in. She knows I will understand her, and in return she tries to understand me. I never have to scold her or say no. If, for example, I'm working on the computer and she comes into in my lap wanting to play, putting her down means "I can't play right now." Okay, says Mimi, and complies.

Mimi extends her communication skills to other people, too. She greets people at the door. She's not afraid of new places. She goes to the office with me—clicks work there, too. She sits on the shoulders of her favorite staff members and watches them type. She's a big hit with strangers because she interacts with them pleasantly at once. She approaches them, she makes eye contact, she tolerates being picked up, and she usually licks them on the nose or chin. They are always surprised and pleased.

The philosopher and dolphin researcher Gregory Bateson once defined clicker training as a method of communicating with an alien species. That it is—most definitely. But it's more.

Once you learn how to communicate with reinforcers, the clicker game becomes part of your worldview. You can't fall back on punishment any more (or at least you can't fail to notice when you do). You have acquired a new and powerful way to develop interactions with others. It begins with reinforcement. It becomes communication and it leads to communion—and that's a good name for love. Perhaps this is what cats have been trying to tell us all along.

CHAPTER

5

Resources:
Where to get help and learn more

Clicker training books, videos, and gear

www.clickertraining.com
Karen Pryor's clicker training headquarters. Training news and articles, clicker community sign-up, email newsletter, clicker Honor Roll (wins and achievements by clicker trained dogs, cats, horses), monthly 'letter from Karen,' archives of Karen's writings on clicker training, links to other clicker Web sites and lists for cats, horses, birds. Secure online ordering for clicker books, videos, and gear, or call 1-800-47 CLICK.

Clicker training gear
*   Sturdy training clickers, three clickers . . . . $ 6.95
    with instructions
*   The folding aluminum target stick . . . . $ 16.95
*   Clip-on clicker; wear on your wrist . . . . $ 7.95
    snap it to a belt, or hang it up

Getting Started clicker kits
Includes instruction book, two clickers, coupons, and treats.
Getting Started: Clicker Training for Cats KIT . . . . $ 16.95
Getting Started: Clicker Training for Dogs KIT . . . . . . $ 16.95
Getting Started: Clicker Training for Horses KIT . . . . . . $ 16.95

Coming soon!
Getting Started: Clicker Training for Birds KIT . . . . . . $ 16.95

Clicker training books
Don't Shoot the Dog! The New Art of Teaching and Training, by Karen Pryor. The 'bible' on reinforcement training, not just for pets but in the classroom, for sports, and in family life. American Psychology Association award winner. Newly revised and enlarged in 1999. 300,000 copies in print. . . . . . $ 12.95

Clicking with your Dog, Step-by-Step in Pictures, by Peggy Tillman. This easy visual guide to over 100 clicked behaviors for dogs is useful for cat owners as well because most clicked behaviors can be trained the same way in either species. 200 pp. . . . . $ 29.95

Clicker training videos
Clicker Magic! 55 min.
Twenty actual clicker training sessions with dogs, puppies, a mule, a fish, and an incredible agility cat. Fun and informative.
VHS (US format) . . . . $ 39.95
PAL (European format) . . . . $ 49.95

Shipping and handling additional on all orders.
To order, call 1-800-47CLICK or visit www.clickertraining.com

Clicker cat Internet sites and lists

www.clickercat.com
A source for articles, archives, and news about new clicker cat books, videos, Web sites. Includes a "Look what MY cat can do" page. Subscribe to this very active cat clicker list for great stories and personal advice from hundreds of other owners of clicker-trained cats.

www.click-l.com
The biggest and oldest clicker list provides a great deal of information mostly but not entirely about dogs. Includes archives and links to other lists and Web sites.

www.animaltrainermagazine.com
Subscribe to this handsome new magazine devoted to modern animal training and training science. Catherine J. Crawmer, editor. . . . . $ 29.95 year.

Appendix

Fifteen Tips for Clicking with Cats

1. Push and release the springy end of the clicker, making a two-toned click. Then treat. Keep the treats small. Use a delicious treat at first: little cubes of roast chicken, say—not a lump of kibble.

2. Click DURING the desired behavior, not after it is completed. The timing of the click is crucial. Don't be dismayed if your pet stops the behavior when it hears the click. The click ends the behavior. Give the treat after that; the timing of the treat is not important.

3. Click when the cat does something you like. Choose something easy at first, that the cat is likely to do on its own. (Ideas: sit, come toward you, touch your hand with its nose, raise a paw, touch a target.)

4. Click once (in-out.) If you want to express special enthusiasm, increase the number of treats, not the number of clicks.

5. Keep practice sessions short. Much more is learned in three sessions of one minute each than in one long session. You can get noticeable results, and teach your cat many new things, by fitting a few clicks a day here and there in your normal routine.

6   If you have more than one cat, separate them for training, and let them take turns.

7   Click for voluntary (or accidental) movements toward your goal. You may coax or lure the cat into a movement or position, but don't push, pull, or hold it.

8   Don't wait for the "whole picture" or the perfect behavior. Click and treat for small movements in the right direction. You want the cat to sit, and it starts to crouch in back: click. You want it to come when called, and it takes a few steps your way: click.

9   Keep raising your goal. As soon as you have a good response—when the cat is voluntarily lying down, coming toward you, or following the target—start asking for more. Wait a few beats, until the cat stays down a little longer, comes a little faster, follows a little further. Then click. This is called "shaping" a behavior.

10 When the cat has learned to do something for clicks, it will begin showing you the behavior spontaneously, trying to get you to click. Now is the time to begin offering a cue, such as a word or a hand signal. Start clicking for that behavior if it happens during or after the cue. Start ignoring that behavior when the cue wasn't given.

11 If your cat does not respond to a cue, it is not 'being stubborn;' it just hasn't learned the cue completely. Find more ways to cue it and click it for the desired behavior, in easier circumstances.

12 Carry a clicker and 'catch' cute behaviors such as rolling, bowing, or holding up one paw. You can click for many different behaviors, whenever you happen to notice them, without confusing your cat.

13 If you get mad, put the clicker away. Don't scold. You will lose the cat's confidence in the clicker and perhaps in you.

14 If you are not making progress with a particular behavior, you are probably clicking too late. Accurate timing is important. Get someone else to watch you, and perhaps to click for you, a few times.

15 Above all, have fun. Clicker training is a wonderful way to enrich your relationship with your cat.

Karen Pryor

About the Author

Karen Pryor is a behavioral biologist with an international reputation in two fields, marine mammal biology and behavioral psychology. Karen was a founder of Hawaii's Sea Life Park, where her work with dolphins pioneered modern, force-free animal training methods. She is the author of *Don't Shoot the Dog! The New Art of Teaching and Training,* a bestseller on training without coercion. She is also the author of several other books and many scientific papers and popular articles on learning and behavior.

Karen Pryor is a founder of "clicker training," a training system based on operant conditioning and the all-positive methods developed by marine mammal trainers. Clicker training is now in use by people working with pet and performance animals of all kinds, and with wild animals in zoos and marine parks worldwide.

Karen has presented clicker training seminars to thousands of pet owners and animal care givers across the US, Canada, Europe, and Japan, as well as giving live clicker training television demonstrations in the US and abroad. She has personally clicker-trained horses, dogs, dolphins, whales, cats, birds, and many kinds of zoo animals. She is the CEO of Sunshine Books, a clicker training publishing and Internet company. She has three grown children and lives in Boston with two clicker-trained dogs and a clicker-trained cat.

For more information about Karen Pryor and clicker training go to www.clickertraining.com